Of My Life

My Journey Through
Difficult Times and Seasons

By Katrina Collins

Dedication

This book is dedicated to my family, loved ones, friends, and anyone who needs healing and/or deliverance in any way, shape, or form. It's also in memory of some very influential people in my life who are no longer here: my father, Howard Collins; my mother, Marie Collins; Mother Mullins; Mother Miller; and Aunt Esther.

A special thank you to Carole, my editor, who has the skill and patience to show me how to write, and then puts everything in context so that it can be understood.

Table of Contents

Table of Contents

(Continued)

Introduction

As I began writing this particular book, I was inspired by the fact that I have a story to tell! Many of us have stories to tell, as a matter of fact, we all have stories to tell, but some of them just don't get written. The point is that I personally believe that this is part of my destiny. It's a part of me that needs to come out and be shared with those who choose to read it.

My first book was inspirational poetry that sometimes rhymed and sometimes didn't. This book isn't only meant to inspire, but also to encourage and uplift the reader.

Every story is unique, including this one. I'm writing this to let you know that whatever you may be going through, you're not alone. As you read this, you may see similarities between my story and yours.

This isn't my entire story, which is why it's called a summary. I pray that many will be blessed by this short but informative account of the different back and forth events of my life.

God bless you all and may the process of healing begin as you read!

Sincerely,

Katrina

Summary of My Life

Chapter 1

A Little Family History

This is my life story. Some things are hard to write about, some things are a little easier. This may be a familiar story to some, but to others it will be entirely new. While there are many others in this story, I'm not only the main character, but also the narrator. When you have a story to tell, no one can tell it like you do!

Let's start with a little history! I was born in Dallas, Texas. I was a big baby at almost 10 pounds, and I'm sure my mother had a hard time with the delivery because of my size!

I have two sisters; one is 10 months younger than me and the other is six years older. My younger sister lives in Minnesota, where I also live, and my older sister lives in Texas, where there are other family members as well.

I have four grown children: two boys and two girls. They have children who have children, so there are four living generations in our family with grandbabies, great grandbabies, nieces, nephews, and cousins too!

I also have extended family that I love just as though they are naturally mine!

My mother and father are both deceased, but they lived full lives well into their 80's, which was a real blessing!

Chapter 2

Growing Up

As a child, my life was interesting, to say the least! There were a lot of children in our neighborhood, and my younger sister and I had a lot of fun playing with just about everybody! She wasn't always happy about it, but my older sister used to watch out for me and my younger sister.

My mother and father both worked hard to provide for us, so we always had what we needed and also a lot of what we wanted! To this very day, I couldn't say whether it was hard or easy for my parents to raise, clothe and feed us, because they didn't talk about it in front of us.

I always assumed that my mother and father really loved each other. They would interact with us, but it didn't seem like they really paid that much attention to each other. I don't know what the actual struggle was for them, but they still made time for us and we felt loved!

Shared Housing

We always had somebody living with us, whether it was family, friends, or just acquaintances. When we lived in a duplex, there were some men who lived upstairs. One of the men, Mr. Holiday, kind of kept an eye on the other men who stayed there.

There was another man, Mr. Tatum, who was so drunk once that he fell down the stairs and made a big hole in the wall. We didn't really think he was too badly hurt, because the plaster was cheap and shallow. He just got up and acted like nothing had happened!

Then there was also a man named Paul, who watched me and my younger sister. One night, he came into our bedroom, when we were already in the bed, and he pulled my gown off my shoulder and kissed me on it! I was so scared that I tried to pretend I was asleep, hoping he would stop and go away! It worked because he left the room. I just thank God that he didn't bother my sister! I never told my dad because I thought he would kill him!

I didn't feel as if my parents weren't protective of us; I just felt they needed some time to themselves. If they'd had any idea that something like this would have happened, they never would have left us alone with that man! To God be the glory; I only remember that happening one time!

Another incident I remember was when my sister and I were coming from the store and a man chased us home. As we got to the front door, my father was standing there, and he asked the man where he thought he was going. The man turned around and ran off. I believe the sound of my father's voice and the look in his eyes scared him off!

I remember when my mother and father used to have parties. Everyone was so drunk that they didn't realize we were drinking their drinks and pretending to smoke their cigarettes, when we were supposed to be cleaning up. We didn't even stop to think about how nasty that was! I was always the one to tell on my sister, and then I acted like I wasn't doing the same thing!

Our Texas Relatives

One summer, we went to Texas to visit some of the relatives on my grandmother's husband's side. When we were pulling a little girl in a wagon, she fell out, so they decided to teach us a lesson about paying attention. One of them dressed up in a devil costume, and he stood at the end of the couch we were lying on. He scared the mess out of us and we were screaming! There were several in the kitchen laughing at us for being so scared! I can laugh at it now, but at the time it wasn't funny at all!

My grandmother would send us care packages with clothing and other things from Dallas. We had cousins living in Texas who were angry with us, because they felt like we thought we were better than them! They also said that my grandmother favored us over them. When we visited them in the summer though, they weren't mean to us and we had fun. Even when we visited our cousins on my dad's side, we always had a good time.

Some Good Memories

Some memories are painful, but not all of them. We were raised in church, and even though I remember some fun times, the importance of walking with God didn't really sink in until I got much older!

My younger sister and I both took piano lessons and were even in a few recitals, but that didn't last long. My sister was so good that she could have become a concert pianist! I only took lessons because my mother was making the decisions and she paid for them.

I was always musically inclined, except when I tried playing the trombone. I didn't know how to control it, and my slide kept coming all the way out. If I lost control, I figured it might hurt somebody if they were too close to me!

I also loved singing and art work growing up, but I didn't seem to be good at anything else. My grades weren't good! How come my sisters got it, but I didn't? I'm not trying to make everything negative; I'm just telling the truth!

My Thoughts on the Matter

I was a sullen, moody child from about five on up. I often played by myself and didn't talk a lot, because I didn't want to be bothered. I didn't believe that anyone cared enough to try and understand my innermost thoughts and feelings. After all, I was just a child, who was very strange and different from either of my sisters!

I had a lot of deep-rooted rage, because of what I had seen, heard, and experienced. Once I sat at the top of the stairs and waited for my younger sister to come upstairs. I threw a wooden block at her, and I also bit her in the side where she had stitches. I was angry with her and I don't even remember why! I had too much anger in me, and I took it out on her most of the time. I just thank God that she doesn't hate me for the way I treated her throughout the years!

I wasn't on any medication to calm me down or improve my behavior. Supposedly, some of us have chemical imbalances, but I do believe that there are better ways to solve that without always having to take some type of medication!

I've also learned that demonization is very real! When Christians speak of deliverance, those who don't believe in it act as if it's some kind of hocus pocus, and that we're trying to do away with the medical profession. Doctors are needed for a lot of reasons, so that's simply not true!

I'm not sure if I had a chemical imbalance or spiritual problem at that time. I also can't say that I was totally withdrawn as a child. I was always a thinker, which can be a good or bad thing, depending upon what you are thinking about!

Chapter 3

The Turbulent Teens

A Divided Family

My sister and I were maybe 12 and 13 when we learned that our parents were getting a divorce. This was devastating to us, as we were completely in the dark about them not getting along! How could this be happening, and how had it gotten to this point? So much was hidden from us! Marriages are supposed to last and families are supposed to stay together! Why didn't or couldn't we? When my mother and father were together, we used to have so much fun with both of them!

There's a ride at the amusement park that spins very fast and the bottom falls out; it feels like you're going to fall, but you're stuck to the side. At that time in my life, I felt that was exactly what was happening!

I no longer felt like I had a solid family foundation! So I did what I did, and I made excuses for my behavior and the choices and decisions I was making! Why was my family the one that had to fall apart? Oh my God, what now?! Even though the tears welled up in my eyes, I felt like I couldn't cry; I could only do that in my private time, when I was alone! No one needed to know or see how badly I had been hurt!

Once my parents got their divorce, I wanted to live with my father. But that didn't happen for whatever reason, and I was very upset about it!

My Rebellion

I began running around, doing all kinds of things, including having sex at the age of 13. I became very disobedient and disrespectful, and I was even going to the bars with my "so-called" friends. Grown men started paying attention to me. Not good!

From the age of about 15, I had sex with several men; sometimes even two or three in one day! It sounds and actually was nasty, but that wasn't my focus when I was doing it. We all have issues in life and sometimes we take them out on others. It doesn't excuse the behavior; it's just one of those sad facts of life!

As the years passed, I spent less and less time paying attention in school and more time doing what I thought I really wanted to do. I was barely getting by in school, but they still passed me to the next grade, until I reached the 12th grade; then I just quit altogether! My sisters applied themselves and got good grades, but I was unconcerned about what type of future I would have without enough education.

Being a teenager was hard for me, because I thought with my body and not with my mind. I didn't drink that much or get high between the ages of 13-18; sex was my drug of choice! Since I had the body, I figured I might as well use it. My actions didn't give me a good reputation, except with the guys, although it really wasn't that good with them either; they just saw it as an open invitation to have sex with them. I didn't have any positive goals in my life. I was running away from home, sleeping around, and sometimes homeless by choice. I was very irresponsible and sexually active, not thinking about what could happen to me if I didn't stop!

For instance, once I was trapped in a house that caught on fire, because the man who lived there was smoking in bed. He must have fallen asleep and dropped his cigarette. It then became a matter of every man for themselves! Not one person warned me to get out of there! It was like nobody cared; if you made it fine, if you didn't...oh well! I believe I was the last one to make it out! I literally had to bust through the back door, which fortunately for me was rusty! I didn't realize then that God's plan for my life didn't include me dying in a fire! As I look back, I just thank God for His grace and mercy!

There's a song that says you always hurt the one you love. That was true in my case, because I hurt my mother so many times with my behavior. I never even considered that I was hurting myself more than anyone else! I was on a collision course, and I wouldn't have listened to anyone anyhow! I was burying my hurt and pain, while allowing my body to be used as an object for pleasure by guys who really didn't care about me, much less love me! I really didn't even love myself then, so what difference did it make if they didn't either? I knew there was a God, but that just wasn't an option for me!

My **Parents**

My mother was very beautiful and my father was very handsome! I have a few pictures of my mother, but none of my father. Sometimes when I think about them, I laugh or smile when I remember something they had said or done!

My father was very fun loving, but my mother was the serious one. Even though she didn't laugh a lot, my mother had a rich, hearty laugh. Whenever she laughed, we knew that whatever she was laughing about was truly funny! It was my mother who usually disciplined us, but my father didn't play and would step in when it was necessary. We tried not to push his buttons!

My father was a hustler, and a good worker and provider! When he hustled, he used to pick people up and take them to and from different places for pay. When he worked, he worked hard at a rubber company, and he was there for many years. When he provided for us, we felt well taken care of.

Things happened, so my parents weren't always able to do everything they wanted to, although they were hard workers and had good jobs! They did teach us the value of working and how to take care of ourselves. My mother and father were both excellent cooks too! I'm sure that's how I learned to cook, and I thank them for that!

My mother never remarried after my father, but my father remarried twice more, as far as I know, and both of the women resembled my mother in some way and were even like her in other ways. Isn't that something? I still wonder if somehow things could have worked out for them. It makes me sad when I think about it! But God knows everything, even before it happens!

I have my own personality, although I did pick up traits from both of my parents. There's a song called "That's the Breaks", and in many aspects of my life, it was like that song was written just for me!

A Word about My Mother

My mother worked hard to provide for my sisters and me, which looking back now I can see. Even though she struggled, she did her best to create and maintain a safe and happy environment, but it began to take a toll on her. My mother had a lot on her plate, but she kept going. As far as we knew, she always paid the bills on time or made arrangements until she was able to take care of them. If she had a hard time with anything, she didn't tell us. I was so self-absorbed that I didn't even give a second thought to what she might be going through! The most reassuring thought that I have about those times was that my mother still loved me, in spite of my obnoxious behavior!

I imagine there were many nights that my mother lost sleep, interceding for me and my safety. She was probably wondering where I was and what I was doing. At some point, I believe she was able to sleep and had ceased worrying. We need to love and appreciate our mothers, even if they don't always do everything we think they should. No matter what you think is wrong with your mother, pray for her. Cherish her while you have her, because you only get one and they aren't here forever!

Alcohol Issues

My mother was a functioning alcoholic for many years. When she was drunk, it temporarily numbed her senses, and the only thing important at the time was another drink! Some of us aren't as strong as others, and life can sometimes drive people to drink or indulge in other addictive behaviors. We all have our own ways of coping; for some it's easy, for some it's harder, and for others, it almost seems impossible!

As the years went by, we all saw how much my mother was drinking and how mean it made her. Sometimes my mother drank to the point of being a staggering, stumbling drunk, who was incoherent and unaware of what was going on around her. She began hiding behind a closed bedroom door from all the hurt, pain, sorrow, disappointment, rejection, and anger, especially associated with family members who only saw her faults and shortcomings, but not their own!

We were good at placing the blame! We didn't stop to think that perhaps we were the reason for a lot of her issues! Family members can be some of your best friends, but often times, your worst enemies! Even now, as I'm writing this, I pray that God would deliver us from passing judgment on others and help us to see that we all need deliverance from something! The saddest part is that we don't stop to think about our actions until it's too late, if we even stop to think about them at all! Lord I ask you to forgive us for being so selfish and shallow!

Summary of My Life

A Word about My Father

My father is the one who actually taught us to care about our outward appearance, because for whatever reason, my mother didn't. This seemed somewhat backwards to me, but I never bothered to ask why either. We were usually sent to a hairdresser, who did a good job as far as the styles, but she always cut our hair. Now a trim would have been fine, but she insisted on cutting it every time. I believe that because she had short hair, she felt everyone else's hair should be short too. My mother finally stopped sending us to her. It was my father who used to take the time to French braid our hair.

My younger sister and I would have breakfast or lunch with our father on the weekends, although we enjoyed spending time with him whenever we could. Sometimes we'd go to wherever my father was staying and would spend time with him and his current girlfriend. There seemed to be a lot of drinking and arguing, and I often felt as though my father really wasn't happy. Either the girlfriend or my dad would buy us stuff, trying to make amends for the situation, but that was just temporary and not a real fix!

When my father played golf with some of his friends, he would take us with him. We would roll down the grassy hills and have so much fun! His friends would always give us money to go to the concession stand. Even though we never learned anything about golf, we got to spend time with our father and always enjoyed being with him.

My Oregon Relatives

To keep me from being sent to a detention center or worse, I was sent to Portland, Oregon to stay with some relatives on my father's side. I had responsibilities there, such as cooking and cleaning that I couldn't refuse to do. I went to the farm with one of my cousins where I learned how to feed the hogs and various other chores. One of my father's sisters that I stayed with was very mean and demanding. I no longer had a choice; I had to do what I was told. I now thank God that she was there to help straighten me out, even though it was a temporary situation. I'm also glad that I got to meet my extended family, as they were very nice. They put up with me, and they showed genuine concern for me.

I stayed with my relatives for the summer, but then I ended up back in Minnesota. Even though my father was living in Portland then, and I wanted to stay with him for a while, it didn't work out that way.

Looking Back

Through the years I felt as though I was a blemish or a blend. There was a commercial on TV where various people were all sitting on a couch. They were all dressed in the same pattern as the couch, so they all blended into the couch, and no one even noticed that they were there! Then there is the blemish, which is something that needs to be removed, because it's unsightly and it just doesn't belong! More often than not, I felt like a blemish!

Sometimes we feel things in ways that others don't understand, and we must somehow learn to express those feelings, instead of bottling them up inside. Otherwise, sooner or later, we just explode, because we can't hold those negative emotions in any longer! Sometimes we hope that someone will notice us and care enough to ask what's going on, but that doesn't always happen! I'm not trying to make this a woe-is-me story. I'm just trying to express some of my life experiences and the resulting emotional turmoil. I'm sure others have lived through similar experiences, whether they choose to share them or not!

As I look back on all my hardheadedness and rebelliousness, I thank God for never giving up on me! Thank you so much God! And even though she had her own personal issues and situations, I know deep in her heart that my mother never gave up on me either! Thank you mama!

So much is coming back to my remembrance Lord God that I need your help to process it all! There were actually some good times during my teen years. Some memories stand out more than others, and as God refreshes things, I will share what I can with the reader. Writing is medicinal for me, and we all need healing of some kind during our lives! A lot of people fall by the wayside, because they don't know how to ask for help. They are often ashamed, discouraged, angry or even fearful of what may happen if they need or ask for help, so they often keep everything deeply hidden inside.

Katrina Collins

The Church Ritual

During my teen years, going to church was a weekly ritual. No matter what was done during the week, on Sunday we went to church. I lived with my mother, she insisted upon it, so it was expected of me.

The preacher could have been talking directly to me, but I wouldn't have known the difference, because I really wasn't paying attention to a word he said. I knew the difference between right and wrong, but at this stage in my life, I was physically but not spiritually in church. I knew who God was, but I still didn't have a real relationship with Him. To me, Jesus was just in a picture on the wall behind the pulpit. I hadn't even stopped to consider that His grace and mercy were the only things keeping me alive.

What I'm writing isn't for me alone; it's also for others who need the healing, deliverance, and freedom that I did and still do. I needed God in my life, but I didn't know where or how to even begin! My life was empty without Jesus, but I wasn't ready to surrender all!

Chapter 4

An Abusive Marriage

In my late teen years, I met and got pregnant by my oldest daughter's father. My first baby was born, and I'm not quite sure how long after she was born that we got married. His mother and my mother, and possibly my father, wanted us to get married, so we did. One of my uncles married us at my mother's house. If they had known that my husband would become an abuser, they probably wouldn't have been so anxious for us to get married! Going through with this wedding was one of the worst mistakes of my life!

The night before the wedding, I was accused of messing around with the best man. I didn't know or even care about him, but I did feel that something wasn't quite right about him. It really hurt that my soon-to-be husband would listen to him lying about me! Instead of setting his best man straight, he punched me in the face, resulting in a swollen jaw! That's when the abuse began.

Katrina Collins

The Abuse Cycle

My husband used to hurl false accusations at me, and I became a live punching bag that he took his frustrations out on. Once again, he accused me of messing around with a man that I didn't even know, and he ended up breaking my nose and blackening both of my eyes. We were separated at that time.

When we were staying at his mother's house in Michigan, females would call him there to play games on the phone. For instance, he was supposed to pick them up from work or meet them somewhere, while they harassed me on a regular basis. When I told him about it, instead of him saying he would take care of it, he told me not to say anything to these women that would cause them to hurt me! I expected him to put them in line, let them know who I was, and tell them to stop harassing me, but that never happened! I also got tired of him putting his hands on me and calling me all kinds of names; he never had anything good to say about me!

I had finally had enough! One of my cousins, who lived close by at the time, gave me enough money for me and my baby to go back to Minnesota. We got on the bus and left!

Unfortunately, my husband returned to Minnesota also and the abuse continued! I had allowed this man to instill so much fear in me that I couldn't shake it off or get free from it! Even his father told me that I didn't have to put up with his continual abuse, and he even offered to pay for a divorce if I wanted one! I never took him up on his offer.

Blatant Abuse

Summary of My Life

By now, my husband was sleeping around with a female not only in our apartment, but in our own bed! That's what I considered the ultimate betrayal!

We lived a few blocks from my mother's house, and my baby and I were there waiting for my husband to come and pick us up. I fell asleep waiting for him, and when I awoke early the next morning, I felt that something wasn't right. Even though it was very early, I got up and walked to the apartment to see what was causing me to feel so uneasy.

When I got there, the chain lock was on the door, but I could see a family friend and his girlfriend sleeping on the couch. When I couldn't get all the way into the house, because of the chain, I became angry and pushed hard on the door. The chain broke and the door opened! I went straight to the bedroom, and my husband was in bed with this female wrapped in his arms. When I woke him up to tell him that I was there, he looked around and pretended not to know what was going on!

I headed for the kitchen and he followed me. I grabbed a knife because I was gonna stab both of them. He wrestled with me until he got the knife out of my hand. Then he pushed me into the closet and removed the loose handle, so I couldn't get out until he had gotten that woman out of our apartment! I don't remember who let me out. I was so hurt at the time that I just wanted to kill both of them! No thought was given then to the consequences or jail time.

I did wonder why I hadn't just gotten the knife and not said anything, but things could easily have been reversed. Instead of me stabbing and killing one or both of them, they could have ended up with the knife, and I might have been killed. I was angry, hurt, frustrated, humiliated, and full of rage! He thought it was a joke!

I don't think my husband ever really loved me. I just believe that he married me to be around our daughter; he really did love her!

In the end, he was struck and killed by a man whose woman he was messing around with. He was at a bar with the woman, her man came in and saw them together, and they got into a fight. My husband beat the man up and they left the bar. When he got home, one of his cousins wanted him to accompany them to the store, so he did. That's when this man saw my husband and ran him over with his car. What a tragic end to his life!

Breaking the Abuse Cycle

This is fact, not fiction; it's real, not sugar coated; it's sometimes hard and cold, but to the best of my recollection, this is just the way it was! We must be careful about how we are living, so that when our lives end, we know where we are going to spend eternity!

If there's any sign of abuse in your relationship, please allow God to work on that person before you ever consider marrying them. If you are already involved in an abusive relationship, then get out of it, allowing the abuser to get the help they need to change! Don't think you can change anyone!

As I'm writing this, my hope is that it will help someone who has gone through or is going through an abusive situation. I don't remember how or even when, but I was finally able to break free from this man, and I thank God that I lived to tell the story!

Chapter 5

A Life at Risk

I was pretty wild and loose in my younger years, but I also didn't have the best attitude or behavior well into my forties. Life is a continuous series of events, which can take us in many different directions. If we did everything the right way, the first time, would we learn anything? Everyone has their own tests and testimony! Not everyone has to learn the hard way, but I did because I was hard headed!

Unintended Callings

A couple of my friends were well-paid prostitutes, and I tried being one for a very brief period of time. When I turned a trick with a man, he gave me $5, put me out of his car, and just left me somewhere. That wasn't the line of work for me! Once again, God's hand of protection was upon me, because I had no idea about what could have happened to me! I could have lost my life trying to do something so foolish!

I even tried my hand at selling weed. The people who were supposed to be selling it for me either smoked it or sold it and kept the money! That wasn't the right business for me either! What made me think that these illegal activities would work?

Unintended Assaults

I have been raped at least four times and by more than one person in succession at least twice! The first time, two guys that I went to school with took me to a place where it happened. I felt pressured into going along with things, but I knew that they would only take me home if I did!

Another time, I was getting a ride home from a friend's husband, and he wouldn't let me out of the car until I gave in. I couldn't fight my way out, because I had my baby in my arms, but he didn't care about that, as long as he got what he wanted. I was afraid to tell my friend, so I told a friend of hers. When he found out that I had told on him, he lied and said that I had come on to him. My friend believed him, and she wouldn't speak to me for years afterwards!

Then there was a group of guys in a cab outside of this bar I was at by myself. I wasn't allowed to wait inside for my cab, because they had closed and I was told to leave. I was standing outside and there was a cab, so I stupidly went up to it and opened the door. Because it was dark, I didn't realize that others were already in the cab. I was taken into an apartment building where I had sex with at least three to four men who took turns with me!

Being raped is one of the worst things that could happen to a woman! You feel like you just can't get clean enough afterwards!

With Great Remorse

This is one of those times where I become weepy, because I remember being hurt to the point of devastation, but I also remember hurting others that seriously too! If we would just stop and think before we hurt others, or even ourselves, a lot of the pain and anguish would cease. Even though these were absolutely horrible experiences, I sincerely thank God for saving my life!

Chapter 6

Relationships

I have been married four times. In Chapter 4, I shared briefly about my first marriage. The other three marriages and the first have one thing in common; all of these men were womanizers! I'm not putting all of the blame on them, because I was an open target, and they could see it all over me. I had itching ears that listened to all their flattering words! It all sounded so good that I fell for it, and no matter what anyone else said, I believed what they told me! Two of them always expected a "yes" from me for everything, and I didn't have the nerve to say no! I believe that they all had feelings for me, but I don't know if it was just lust or infatuation!

Husband #2 divorced me while he was still in prison! I found out about the divorce almost two years after the fact, but I wasn't angry with him. Even though I didn't know about it, I wasn't really surprised!

I never should have pursued husband #3, because he was like a ticking time bomb waiting to go off! There were too many emotional and even mental issues involved in that relationship. The actual marriage was like walking through a mine field; there could be an explosion at any moment, if you stepped on a hot spot! I got what I got because I did what I did!

I rushed into marriage with husband #4, because I thought it was my last chance at marriage, but it was over in less than a year! At the time, the Holy Ghost had told me to wait at least six months before making the decision to marry this man! Had I listened, I wouldn't have made that mistake!

I never sought God concerning any of these marriages, and that's one of the reasons I encountered such terrible situations with all of them! Everything that happened was due to my disregard for doing the right thing! We aren't supposed to marry just to marry; it's supposed to be a lifelong commitment!

God still speaks to us through the Holy Ghost, ordinary people, and variety of other ways, but how often do we really listen? The fact of the matter is that I heard from God, but a lot of times I would ignore or second guess what I had heard. I don't think that was a good or smart thing to do, but that's what got me into many situations that only God could get me out of! He still came to my rescue and gave me a way of escape! I just thank God over and over for forgiving me, in spite of my foolishness and determination to do things my way!

Several years ago, husband #1, the father of my oldest daughter, passed away. The rest of these men are still alive, and I pray they are living happy and prosperous lives! Forgiveness goes both ways and I pray that the feeling is mutual!

The Lie of Living Together

As far as living with someone before marriage, it didn't work for me because playing house isn't of God and there are consequences. Even though I ended up marrying three of those men, it didn't last because it started off wrong.

In one of these relationships, we lied to people and told them that we were married before it even happened. We weren't even engaged at the time and he was still married. I stupidly went along with the lie, knowing that we were lying in the sight of God! In the Bible, people have fallen down dead for lying! I just thank God for not striking me dead in my sinfulness! When I say praise the Lord, I really mean it!

Then I met a man who was younger than me and began a relationship with him. It wasn't too long before he moved in with me, and the roller coaster ride began again. I was playing house once more! I was so stubborn and rebellious that I refused to see the red lights or hear the sirens going off in my head! I thought I knew what I was doing this time, but I was WRONG...another abuser!

Men can be abusers, but so can women; it can go both ways! I can't and won't blame everything on the men. I refused to look at the facts, which should have been very apparent to me by now. I only paid attention to what I wanted to see! I thought I could handle all of these situations, but I definitely got in over my head! My choices weren't good, so I kept getting involved with womanizers!

I was the type that when everything was falling apart in my relationship or marriage, I wanted everyone to come to my rescue, but when I went back to playing house or was on the fake and short-lived honeymoon, I didn't want to be bothered by anybody! If you're paying attention, I hope that you learn to discern the real from the fake!

Faulty Perceptions

There were times in my life when I linked sex and love together. I dressed in a way that I thought would get attention, but what I failed to realize was that the way I was dressing wasn't who I really was. It was very suggestive and sending all the wrong signals!

We become silly foolish women, who allow words to make us feel better when what we really want are words with action behind them. I was one of those women who had no real sense of being valued as a person, and I allowed my emotions to mislead me time after time. We may think we are in a real relationship, but if sex comes first, or it's all we have in common, it's not of God and self is definitely in charge! God doesn't send us someone to sin with!

I loved hard and fell hard, because more often than not I didn't meet the expectations of the man I was with at the time. Sex was all we had in common, and once that was over, we really didn't have another way of interacting, so we both just went our separate ways until the next time.

Sex was our common ground. I'm not making excuses for what I did, but it was a doggy dog existence. I had the body, so I really didn't need much of a mind, and the saddest part of it all was that I put myself in that position! I was used and I used in return. I had no sense of worth or morals! For a lot of years, I was just a sex object and not much of a human being. I had no self-esteem, whether by choice or condition, and I was trapped in a life of sex, drugs, abuse, and haywire mindsets for many years!

Good and Bad Relationships

Everything in life has a season. Sometimes those seasons are brief, some are long lasting, and some are even for a lifetime! Some relationships cause us to learn something, some are to teach something, but some go much deeper than that! Whether it's to learn about the reality of it, to teach about our levels of expectation in it, or to go deeper in all areas concerning it, we need wisdom and understanding about relationships!

I didn't really know how to discern the difference between a good or bad relationship. I thought I had to work at making things better or lasting. However, a relationship is between two people, and both parties have to want the relationship to work and last!

A real relationship starts off with getting to know one another. We learn the other person's likes and dislikes, their visions and goals, how to have patience with the other person, in spite of any differences, and how to agree to disagree. Going places and doing things together causes you to grow as one. It's no longer always about what I want to do, but what are we going to do.

If you first like and then learn to love someone, you can more easily weather the storms together. For some reason, I believe that the lines of communication had broken down between my parents. I didn't want that to happen to me, because I've already been there and done that too many times!

I've had many casual sexual relationships that didn't amount to much. I also had some serious relationships, or so I thought, that didn't amount to much. Either I really cared about them, but it wasn't mutual or they cared about me, and it wasn't mutual on my part! Either I got serious too quickly and they ran off, or they got serious too quickly and I ran off! No matter how a relationship did start out, I felt that one day everything would change, and it would become what I expected it to be. But as long as I went at it this way, nothing would ever change the way it needed to. My whole outlook on being a woman had been distorted for too many years. Yes, there are men who will use us regardless, but there are also men who genuinely care if we have a mind and not just a body!

Looking back, I never really wanted to be the head in a relationship. But more often than not, I was left to fend for myself and my children, so I didn't have much of a choice. I found myself in the place where I had to buy the groceries and pay the bills, putting me in the role of provider. I felt like I had to do what I did in order to be in a relationship. I never stopped to think that even if I did all of this, they eventually would leave, and that's exactly what happened! The way I went into a relationship and the way it ended weren't the way it was supposed to be!

A real relationship and marriage are both of great value! If you don't know the difference, then ask God, and He will show you the difference. Anything worth having needs to be built upon, and as it grows, it needs to be nurtured and maintained. As I said before, both the man and woman must be willing to work on their relationship, if they want to have a good one. We also need to realize that relationships aren't like fairy tales; there's no magic formula in real life!

Getting Real

Until we are old enough to care for ourselves, life is basically pretty easy, because we don't have any responsibilities. We are children doing what we are told and in the process of just growing up! I pray that for those who've had a childhood harder than others! As they continue to grow, may God work it out for them!

A lot of us say that we wish we were grown up, so we could do whatever we want to. But when we are grown, we begin to see that our parents are no longer responsible for us. Now we have to pay our own rent and bills, buy food and clothing, and whatever else goes along with being an adult! Now we really need to look to God who is our source! Look at it this way, He will make a way when it seems like there is no way!

In spite of all the things that I've experienced, I'm still a firm believer that love is wonderful! Everyone needs somebody to love who will love them in return! Women need to be affirmed and men want to be respected! It's good to have someone in your life who:

- Enjoys things about you that others may think are silly or ridiculous.
- Pays attention to your moods, passions, and everything that you're about.
- You can let your guard down around.
- Doesn't try to change you, but if you want to change, they will help you through it.
- Knows you well enough to play and joke around with and you don't get offended, and
- Doesn't think we're making fun of them when someone else is present.

Summary of My Life

Relationships and marriages shouldn't be a performance measured on a scale of 1-10! When it comes down to it, how many of us are ever considered a 10; and even if we are, how long does that last? We need values and morals, but most of all we need love!

Life is so precious and full of mysteries with new things to be discovered daily, whether we realize it or not! We must learn to live life to its fullest, every moment that we can, and embrace it all!

Relationships are a Part of Life

One of the hardest things for me to do was to face life head on from day to day! I had done so much damage to myself and hurt those who loved and cared about me so many times that it was hard for me to believe there was still hope for me!

I have often wondered if it was too late for the right mate to come along, but then I remember that what seems impossible with man is still and always possible with God! As long as I have breath in my body, it's never too late for God to send me a husband! I just have to be patient, because God knows who the right one is for me.

I believe that I'm now ready for marriage, and I also believe that God is preparing me for my mate! I know I will have to allow him to get to know me, as I get to know him. I'm not talking about just falling for a man, because he seems to show interest in me. I've been there and done that too many times already. I'm talking about true wisdom and discernment to know, and not keep guessing about, whether it is or isn't the right man for me! I really do want a husband, but this time I want a marriage that will last! I don't believe that we are ever too old for real love!

I hope the man who finds me will believe that I'm very valuable, and he will love me as Christ loves the church! We can't choose our family, but we can choose our friends and ask for guidance with our soul mates. We also need wisdom and understanding in all of our relationships. I didn't really know how to relate to my family, and it turns out that I didn't know how to deal with friendships or male and female relationships either.

I want to be able to help maintain and do my part to insure that my marriage will be healthy and have a sustainable balance for my husband and myself. I pray that we won't make any unreasonable demands on one another. It's not always going to be easy to expose different things about myself to a man, but I pray I won't feel that he's trying to hurt my feelings when we disagree. I don't want to be hurt again, so I also pray that I will know the difference between concern and disregard.

God already has and is still delivering me from a lot of baggage, and I pray that He will continue to do so! Thank you God for deliverance! I know that no two relationships are alike, but I also know that we can learn from those who have successful marriages. It's okay to ask questions without seeming to be nosey. Being secretive and hiding things from the beginning is a bad way to start a marriage.

If you truly want to spend the rest of your life with a mate, you have to be able to talk to that person about anything. They might not always understand you and vice versa, but you owe it to yourselves to at least try! My desire is that we will love each other enough to work through the difficult times!

Chapter 7

My Four Children

In Name Only

I've had four children with four different fathers. Each time I became pregnant, I foolishly thought that this was the right man! I also remember thinking that this was finally the relationship that would last! I was truly a foolish and silly woman! My children were the only thing that lasted!

I used to leave my children with my mother and younger sister a lot. As a matter of fact, they raised them while I was out on the streets doing whatever I did! My children needed a mother's love and attention, but all I thought about was me!

Throughout these years of being a mother in name only rather than in reality, I put myself in many compromising situations. Some could even have resulted in death! Although I didn't recognize or give credit where it was due, the hand of God was on my life. Only His grace and mercy kept things from being worse than they were!

Baby Girl # 1

Baby Girl #1 was born when I was in my late teens. I later married her father, who was an abuser, as described in Chapter 4. This is the only one of my children's fathers that I married. I wasn't married to the fathers of my other three children. Husbands #2, #3 and #4 were stepfathers.

Baby Boy #2

Somewhere along the way, I started drinking and smoking weed, and then I got pregnant and had Baby Boy #2. His father was an abuser both physically and mentally. Before I realized that he was an abuser, I had gotten a place and he had moved in with me. What I had backwards was playing house! It never works!

During this time, I became best friends with my neighbor downstairs. She was also going through a lot relationship wise. We regularly spent time encouraging and looking out for each other. Oftentimes, we would even feed our children together. We don't talk very much anymore, but I still love her and consider her my friend and sister!

Before I finally left, this man was seeing another woman, and he took my daughter and son and tried to keep them. But I called my uncle, he and his son (my cousin) came over, and they convinced him to return the children to me. At the time of this writing, the father of my oldest son had recently passed away.

Baby Girl #3

As time went on, I became pregnant with Baby Girl #3 by daddy number three. Sex had already gotten me caught up twice, so why did I believe that this man was the right one? He had a woman when I became pregnant, so what made me think that he would leave her? He got mad when he found out that I was pregnant and denied my daughter for many years!

I really think it's a sad situation when a father denies his own child, because it does take two. It's also sad when a father wants to be a part of their child's life, but the mother doesn't allow it, because the children aren't with her or for whatever other reasons!

Baby Boy #4

In my early thirties, I became pregnant again. Wow! Baby Boy #4 and daddy number four, but that's what happens when you keep sleeping around! You either get diseases, pregnant, or maybe even both! The best birth control is not to have sex!

I had so much going on that I was unable to handle by myself, and then I had to deal with each one of my children's fathers who also had their own issues. But all I thought about was having a good time! The lust of the eyes and the flesh!

I was still going to church then, but I had no real relationship with God, or I would have done much better! I needed Jesus in my life, but I still wasn't ready to let go and seek God! I didn't have time for God, even though He had saved and protected me all this time!

I was now responsible for four more lives besides my own; I was the mother of two girls and two boys!

MIA

Because of my missing-in-action attitude, behaviors, and mindset, my children were deprived of the most fundamental relationship that they deserved for many years! I missed out on most of their birthday parties, events at school, and other celebrations as they grew up!

My oldest daughter missed me and really needed me to be there for her! The other children loved and missed me too, but she was the one who watched out for the younger ones daily! She needed release and a mother to talk to!

Oftentimes, we don't stop to think about how important a mother's love truly is! A father's love is important too, but most of the time, and in most cases, it's the mother who primarily cares for, nurtures, and spends time with the children.

I'm surprised that my oldest daughter even had children later in life, because she really was the big sister with a lot of responsibility concerning the younger ones! My children understandably had a lot of rejection and abandonment issues growing up!

Summary of My Life

The Good in the Bad

There were many fun times and happy memories in my life, not just hard times! When my children were with me, we used to like watching movies and eating popcorn! We also liked having barbeques, because family would come over with all their kids! For the most part, there was never a dull moment! You could feel genuine love during those times!

When she was younger, my mother loved doing things that were never dull or boring. She enjoyed going to concerts, plays and other social events. Once, she was even in a school play with my children, although they didn't really like it at the time! As they look back on it now that she's gone, it's at least something interesting to talk about!

Reflecting Back

As I reflect back on the ages of 20 to 30, I had four children that I didn't know how to properly raise. I had no idea who I could turn to, in order to find out how to become the kind of mother that they would love and respect! Having children isn't to be taken lightly! They need to be nurtured, taught, and loved!

Children should be planned for and anticipated, not just suddenly here! Even though we can't foresee the future, there should at least be some type of financial planning in place, so they can be provided for!

I missed a lot of my children's lives as they grew up, but I can't go backwards! I can say from experience though that you need to pay attention to your children. Every stage of their growing up should be just as important to you as it is to them!

We also have to be careful what we speak over our children! When we see and say that they are different, we must learn how to speak positive versus negative things into the atmosphere over their lives. Words not only build up and edify, but they can also tear down, making them feel worthless and empty inside! Regardless of how they got here, children need to know that they are a blessing and not a curse!

My children are all very intelligent, as well as unique individuals! I pray that they will continue to strive to be all that they can be!

Chapter 8

Influenced by Drugs

This will sound ridiculous, but when I was a young girl, I ate almost a whole bottle of children's orange-flavored aspirin. My grandmother made me walk around a bush in her front yard numerous times, so I would stay awake. I ate all that aspirin because it looked and tasted like candy!

Looking back on that situation now, the lesson I learned was that everything that looks or tastes good isn't necessarily good for you! If we don't get the lesson right the first time, we are destined to go around and around until we get it right, no matter how many times it takes! I also learned that my life depends upon the decisions that I made not only then but now!

Drugs and Marriage

I did drugs with and around two of my husbands. Husband #2 was the one who actually got me started on drugs, but I can't blame him for that fact that I didn't have the will power to say no! He also taught me how to cook dope. When he left me at home for long periods of time, I would cook some dope and get high by myself. It wasn't a smart thing to do, because it just made the addiction worse, but it was an excuse to continue doing it. This actually went on for a while, it wasn't a good thing, but it's what I did to make up for him being gone!

Husband #2 was the one who divorced me while he was in prison, as mentioned in Chapter 6.

When I married Husband #3, I had been delivered from drugs. I foolishly thought that loving and marrying him was enough to make him decide to stop using drugs! On the other hand, we can't change anybody or stop them from doing anything that they really want to do! He had to want to stop on his own. Our marriage didn't change him, but it did change me!

Husband #3 once said that if he found out that I was getting high, he would leave me! He probably thought that I would expect him to share his drugs or that he would have to support my habit as well as his own!

He didn't even know that I got high at first. In the house we lived in at that time, I used to go into the bathroom, raise the window, and blow smoke out of the window, or I would go down in the basement when I figured everyone else was asleep. His threat didn't stop anything, because I paid for my own habit. Nevertheless, we were both destroying our lives with drugs!

Now here I am again, finding myself angry, frustrated and upset more with myself than Husband #3. Once again, I had done things my way, instead of seeking God before jumping into another marriage! It really is important to seek God before making decisions that have serious and sometimes even fatal consequences! I thank God that my consequences weren't fatal, although they were still serious!

I can't even begin to explain the feelings I had inside when I saw other people's marriages working and mine ending the way that they did. I know marriage is a two-way street and both the man and the woman have to work at it. But why couldn't I just get it right according to God's plan and not mine?

Drugs Out of Control

In my thirties, after I had my youngest son, I began to really use and abuse drugs out of control! I took off and went to Chicago with a man that I barely knew. I met this man while he was locked up. When he got out, we were smoking dope and got on a Greyhound bus to Chicago. We went to his mother's house, and even though it was already full, we still stayed there.

I don't remember exactly how long I was in Chicago. It was absolutely ridiculous, because I didn't have any business being there in the first place! Before I had sense enough to go home, this man punched me in the right eye so hard that it felt like he had knocked it out of the back of my head! I guess God was still looking out for me, in spite of my unwillingness to surrender!

Drugs and Finances

Once again, I was back at my mother's house! I got a job and every time I got paid, I would smoke dope and spend all of my money on it. When I ran out of money, the people who sold me the dope kept letting me smoke until I owed them all of my next check!

I even spent the rent money that I owed on the house I was living in, which happened to be my mother's. I had taken over the payments when she moved into another house. And because of my addiction, I lost the house! Everyone who stayed there was doing whatever they did, but they were all following my example! So many memories were lost with that house, some good and some bad!

There were times when I had to walk 22 blocks to work in the snow, because I had spent all of my money getting high over the weekend, and I was totally broke! I had a supervisor who would give me money to get back and forth to work until payday came around, with no questions asked. I believe she knew what was going on, but she never said anything! She recently passed away. I pray that she made peace with God!

Drugs with a Friend

My best friend and I used to smoke weed day and night, drink Lambrusco, and eat everything in sight! We thought that was okay, but it really wasn't! I don't care if pot is legal now! Anything you put in your body that alters your mental or physical capabilities isn't good for you, and the consequences still remain to be seen!

Just like medications that we take, I believe that some of these drugs, including alcohol, can have devastating side effects, causing changes inside the body which could eventually lead to death! I'm thankful that I didn't die in my addiction, although some didn't make it!

Drugs and Family

My life was in shambles and here I was moving in with my mother again! My mother had allowed us to drink around her when we were old enough, but I went way too far when I not only let my children drink around me, but I also smoked weed with them! I wasn't a good example of what a mother should be! I was too busy trying to be their friend and a bad one at that! Would I ever become the example that my children needed me to be?

Drugs and Health

I did a lot of things in my life to get attention. I played sick a lot, but then I really began to get sick and started having issues in my body. I even pretended to commit suicide once. I took a razor and put surface cuts on my wrists, but I couldn't go through with it. I really didn't want to kill myself!

Over the years, sometimes I would get so high that I thought my heart would stop or it had even stopped beating. That was so crazy, because how could I even think if my heart had stopped and I was no longer breathing? Instead of stopping the drugs though, I just kept on getting high!

One time when I was heavily on drugs, I was really sick and decided to get high anyway. I became so sick that I thought I was going to die! I kept laying down and getting back up, walking the floor, and praying that I would come down and still be alive!

It was really something that when I was high, I could pray to sober up, but when I wasn't high, I hardly ever prayed! The last time I got high smoking dope, I went into the bathroom, and when I looked in the mirror, I saw a black skeleton! The Holy Ghost told me that if I ever got high again, that would be me! It scared me so bad that I had no choice but to stop!

God and Drugs

Throughout my years of addiction, I snorted, smoked, took uppers and downers, prescription drugs, over-the-counter drugs, and I even drank methadone and got so sick from it that I thought I was going to die! God brought me out of every form of addiction, because only He knew what it would take to stop me!

If I could go back and do some things all over again I would, but the hands of time cannot be turned back. In all that we do, there's a measure of faith whether it's good or bad. Nobody does everything right all of the time, but life consists of striving to do the right thing!

Only God could and did save me from totally destroying myself in a life of drug addiction. I'm ever so grateful to God that I didn't have to die in order for it to stop! I thank Him for saving me again and again and again!

Chapter 9

Finding God

Who Am I?

One time I broke down so badly that I literally felt, from the inside out, that I would never be able to function rationally again; and the pain, which was very deep down in my soul, would never be gone! At that time, I really didn't even want to step back into reality!

I saw a movie once where an actor had amnesia. When he woke up, he couldn't remember anything, and he kept asking, "Who am I?" As he kept repeating himself, they thought it was his name, and they started calling him "Who am I". With all that I was going through at the time, I began to question and even wonder...who am I?

Our minds are all patterned differently and work in ways unique to each individual. I just thank God for restoring me to my right mind! I'm sure none of us ever want to be in that place where our minds can't think, reason, or comprehend!

When all the inward battles erupt like a machine gun continuously firing, we must remember that we are still victorious! There are so many ways to handle these life situations, although I didn't know much about them at the time. Please consider that immediate family may not be in a position to help you through things, because they may be going through their own battles too! Don't get angry or give up! I just pray for all those who need help, that they would be inspired to seek Godly counsel!

My Church History

When I was still young, my family went to the Methodist church. In my 20's, I attended the Baptist church. In my 30's and 40's, I went back and forth between the two. In my late 40's and 50's, I attended a nondenominational church.

I really began to pay attention when I started attending the nondenominational church, and things began to slowly change for me. At first, I still had a worldly mentality, and I was smoking weed and drinking, amongst other things! I was just surviving Monday-Saturday and attending church on Sunday. Right after the church service was over, I went right back to doing the same old things! This went on for countless years, with a few changes here and there, until I finally got tired of existing just to survive!

When I joined the church, it was an emotional decision, which should never be the reason for joining a church! I began to be in and out, back and forth, being led by my emotions instead of having an unyielding decision of the mind and heart. Throughout the years, I had started and stopped so many things that it had become a way of life for me. I was inconsistent and didn't follow through with what I had started. There were so many things that I had left undone for too long, and more often than not, I felt overwhelmed and just gave up on a lot of things, accomplishing very little or nothing at all! It took me a long time to realize it, but I just needed Jesus!

The testimony that we speak from our lips is meaningless, if we are saying words just because they sound good! I expected people to believe my words, simply because they sounded so good! What other people think or believe is really unimportant, but I hadn't stopped to think about that! What does matter is what God says and knows about us! He knows the genuine article from the counterfeit; you can't really hide anything from Him!

One of the churches that I went to began to help me to see who I was in Christ, and what I was capable of doing. I consequently became an active member of the church. I was on the praise team, I became a choir member, an intercessor, a prayer warrior, part of the healing ministry, and eventually part of the deliverance ministry.

As my life began to change, I was better equipped to handle all of the situations and circumstances that arose. Things still happened, but now I knew that God would help me get through whatever came my way!

Giftings

When I first joined the church, I was initially shy and reserved, but as time went on, I began to realize who I was becoming in Christ and the gifts began to manifest!

For a long time, I didn't understand what being prophetic was really about! I have dreams and visions, some I remember and some I don't. If it's something I really need to know, I ask God to bring it back to my remembrance, and He's faithful to do so! God now uses me in those areas that He has chosen to gift me with. It still astonishes me, but it's all for His glory!

I loved to sing and still do, and I was even in a band at one time! We were all very talented, but we also had drug, or alcohol issues, and some had both, which kept us from doing anything big with our music. We only played around town, and sometimes we had a wedding reception here and there. We had to divide the money between six or seven people, so the pay really wasn't very good. At one of these events, I met a Pastor who told me that one day I was going to be singing for the Lord, which eventually came to pass!

A New Creation

I have come a long way since the Lord came into my life! When I used to go out with my friends, I didn't have much to say, and the people we were out with thought that I was strange. They would even comment on my strangeness while I was sitting right there! I masked what I was feeling on the inside, because of how people responded to my quietness on the outside!

They had no clue as to what God had in store for me, but at that time, neither did I! More often than not, people try to size you up by the way you look on the outside. As the saying goes, "You can't judge a book by its cover"! That says a lot, because sometimes our physical appearance is totally different from what we are really like inside! The difference in me now is that I no longer have anything to hide! I still have a long way to go, but I'm striving to continue my pursuit of God!

Once we truly come into salvation, things change, but in a good way. Anything worth having doesn't come easily, it's not going to just drop into our laps, and we'll have to work for and at it! Years and layers of faulty mindsets, bad habits, obstinate ways, and everything that doesn't give God glory, must be stripped away! We have to get to the place where we allow God to change us, in order for us to become more like Christ! He's always pruning and shaping me! I glorify you God for picking me up, turning me around, and helping me to become a Godly daughter! Thank you God!

Now I look forward to serving God. Because of His grace and mercy, I can get up and face the day! I may not know everything that's going to happen during the day, but I'm no longer anxious about it. I now live with an expectation that something good is going to happen in thought, word, or deed daily.

Finding a Church Home

I was lost for a very long time, but now I genuinely wanted to change, so I made the decision to find a new life in Christ! I was no longer led emotionally. I had a new mindset, and the desire of my heart had changed, so I could follow Christ now for real!

Being in the company of like-minded people does help, but the most important lesson that I learned was about my need to know God as my Father and Jesus Christ as my Savior! It's all about a personal relationship with Him!

Until we seek God about a church home, we will be undecided, unfulfilled and unsure about our role in the body of Christ. We also won't be making the best choices for ourselves, as we need to have a sense of purpose in our lives that only God can give us.

We all need to be rooted and grounded in a church home somewhere. If you ask God, He will show you where you need to be. The search may start out by going to different churches, but somewhere along the way, God will show you exactly where you need to be.

When choosing a church home, keep in mind that it's not just about how good the praise team is, or how the choir sounds, or if everything makes you feel good! It's about learning the truth of God's Word and making sure it's being preached and practiced. God's Word is alive and active and follows you wherever you go! It's a vital part of your daily life, not just something that's only experienced at church on Sundays! God's Word will help, sustain, and encourage you daily through the difficult times!

Knowledge isn't to be wasted or taken for granted. As I grow older, I thank God for continuing to increase my knowledge. There's a lot to share in God's Word, but we need to know what we are talking about, so that others will understand when we share it with them! If we never read our Word, how is that even possible?

For all those who prayed for me, encouraged, counseled and inspired me, and answered all the questions that I finally had the nerve to ask, I say thank you! God bless and keep you always! I haven't mentioned any names, but you know who you are by the Spirit! I can't thank any of you enough!

Prayer

I used to think that prayer was just for those who used big words or could pray for a long time. Then one day, I realized that when you sincerely come before the Lord, He will teach you how to pray. How long that prayer lasts is between you and the Lord; much can be done in a little time, just as little can be done in much time.

Prayer is a privilege and an honor, and it's truly a gift that we can come before the throne of God with our petitions! Ask the Holy Ghost for direction, because when we don't know what to pray for in the natural, the Holy Ghost will pray through us! If you really want a prayer life, God is faithful and will generously give it to you, if you just ask!

I have prayed for the leadership, as well as the body of Christ, in the different churches that I have attended or been a member of. Praying is an awesome gift from the Lord, and prayer works in both the spirit and natural realms. I can tell you from personal experience that God really does answer prayer! I have experienced and witnessed the manifestation of the power of God in prayer! Glory to God! We must learn how to pray and cry out to the Lord!

Alone Time

When Jesus spent time alone, He was able to hear from and talk to God, giving us a pattern we can follow. We are accustomed to all the daily hustle and bustle around us, and we are often afraid to get to know ourselves when we're alone, but it's important that we learn to love ourselves too!

We don't have to be alone all of the time, but it's important to at least have some alone time for yourself! This was hard for me at first, because I was used to being around family, friends, or acquaintances all or most of the time! It took a long time for me to learn how to be alone but not lonely.

On the contrary, we can be in a room full of people and still feel alone! In those times, we may feel useless, neglected, or even perceived as a nuisance. We can also feel slighted when we think that no one is paying attention to us! We must learn to be comfortable and confident enough with ourselves to be alone at times, even if we are with people.

It's also important that we learn balance in our lives! Our family is also a part of our ministry, and God wants us to enjoy our lives too. When we get saved, it's not all fire and brimstone, and everything is going to send you to hell! We have to ask for discernment and make the right choices to live a life pleasing to God! Life isn't a joke, but there are times to be serious and times to have fun!

Change Me Lord!

Sometimes I would sit and wonder what God's ultimate plan was, and still is, for my life. God doesn't force Himself upon us; we must make the decision as to when or even how we invite Him into our lives. When we do, He's faithful to complete what He has started!

As we begin and continue to have a relationship with Christ, we become better equipped to handle what was once devastating or overwhelming to us! Now with the help of God our Father, Christ our Savior, and the Holy Ghost our Comforter, we can gain or regain a sound mind, have healthy relationships, and learn how to maintain stability in our lives! I can't speak for anyone else, but I know I did and still do need these things in my life! I no longer want my mind and thoughts to be all over the place!

God I need your help to change my mind, so I can see myself the way that you see me. There are so many things that I have overlooked and didn't want to face about myself throughout the years! In reality, we must see our worth and value through His eyes of love, the way we were meant to be seen. I'm an asset to my family, community, and church. This isn't meant in a cocky or prideful way, but in a positive way. To God be the glory!

Healed and Delivered

I've had quite a few mental, soulful, physical, and spiritual issues that I've been healed and delivered from. Some of them I brought upon myself, and some of them I thought I would never be able to get over or through. I've had heart problems, breathing issues, blood clots, other physical conditions, and even some mental issues. But God has delivered me and set me free from a lot of them, and He isn't through with me yet!

I thank God that I still have a life to live, a mind to think, and a heart to forgive! The path I chose to follow for so long not only hurt me, but also my family, other loved ones, and even friends along the way. I'm sure some of them knew of my trials, but they couldn't stop me, and it probably hurt them to see me like that!

When I was a drug user and self-abuser, I was so self-absorbed that I only thought about myself. Just me! I didn't care about anything except getting high, whether it was drugs, alcohol, or even sex. It didn't matter to me that all of these things consumed my entire day and night, although I didn't always enjoy them at times! They had sadly become habits that were hard for me to break! I don't remember the second, minute, hour, or day of my deliverance, but suddenly I no longer desired these things. I was finally free!

Thank God for providing me with healing and deliverance! He has set me free and gives me the liberty to do His will. Change generally doesn't take place overnight; it's a process and that takes time. We get through one situation and then something else comes along. There's always something that we need God to remove from within us.

When we ask God to reveal even the hidden and secret things to us, all of a sudden He shows us residue of something that we thought was over and gone, but it's still there! We may even question why it's still there. For instance, my older sister used to watch out for me and my younger sister when we were growing up. From the conversation we had after my mother passed away in her 80's, my sister still seemed very unhappy about that situation, after all these years! But I believe there were things that happened to her over the years, which she never quite got over; and I can say the same thing about my younger sister too. I know that God is still healing me, and I pray that He will heal them both from the inside out too! I love both of my sisters, in spite of our differences, and I pray that one day they will forgive me for whatever hurt, pain, or stress I may have caused them!

Thank You Lord

Life can be like a never-ending maze that we can't seem to get out of! Or if we do manage to find our way out, it may take what seems like forever! Getting off track isn't the most rewarding way to live, but getting back on track takes effort and determination. I see this time in my life as a high point, not a low one. Even though things may not be the way they will ultimately be, I'm encouraged, because I know it's only going to get better!

We often turn out to be our own worst hindrance! Sometimes I feel sad about the fact that I didn't pay attention to some things sooner, which might have made an overall difference in my life!

Many people offer unsolicited advice, but it's not always the right or even the best advice. Some of them don't really care about you, and some even want to see you fail! For those reasons, it's important that we not only seek, but learn to listen to *wise* counsel! Ask God for His wisdom to know what to do, when to do it, and how it should be done. When you ask, He will also provide Godly counselors for you!

I thank God for providing a roof over my head, clothes on my back, food to eat, and the strength to clean my dwelling place! I'm also so grateful to God for blessing me, so I can be a blessing to others. I thank God for my family near and far, natural and extended.

Every day of life that God continues to give to me, I'm more and more grateful and thankful that He never gave up on me! I always try to remember to thank Him for peaceful rest at night, and the joy of waking up in the morning. No matter what's going on during my day, I love the sunshine, because it always makes me feel so good! Thank you God for the sunshine!

God continued to keep me and saved me for such a time as this! Today, I'm grateful for the fact that the Lord allowed me to live to tell this part of my story!

"Therefore I say to you, her sins, which are many, are forgiven, for she loved much. But to whom little is forgiven, the same loves little." Luke 7:47 (NKJV)

Chapter 10

Lessons Learned

I just recently turned 65, and as I am writing this book, I want you all to know that I have learned a lot of lessons along the way! Some of these lessons, I should have paid attention to a long time ago! But I do thank God that, as long as He allows me to live, I still can learn!

The Holy Ghost told me that my life was just beginning when I turned 56 and I believe it! What I've learned wasn't just for myself, but for others as well! Please don't get it twisted that your lot is to go through things until you reach your latter years!

Not everyone has to or will necessarily do things the same way! I encourage you to pay attention as you read and learn from it! You don't have to go through everything that I did, it doesn't have to be that difficult, and you certainly don't have to be stubborn, rebellious, or disobedient!

Now if you are determined to do things your own way, no matter what advice you receive, well then go ahead. When we refuse to listen, it could cost us our souls, and that's a very expensive price to pay!

Why I Write

I really enjoy writing, and as I write, I'm asking God to allow the reader to enjoy it as much as I do. I don't want to write fiction. I want to be a writer of truth that holds the reader's interest. I try to make my writings meaningful in a way that others can somehow relate to, because I want the reader to feel as though they are experiencing what they are reading. When I begin to write, God downloads in me, and as I put the words on paper, they become alive. I'm blessed to be the bearer of the pen of a ready writer.

I've wanted to write this book for a long time, and I just realized that it finally is the right time! The unique thing about my story is that it's not a carbon copy of someone else's life. It's probably not the most unusual story ever written, but it's about what actually happened in my life!

Choose the Right Leader

I was a follower and not a leader in junior high school, but I wasn't following the right people! I didn't stop to think for myself, so I ended up in trouble and was eventually put out of school. At that time in my life, the negatives outweighed the positives! I knew the difference between right and wrong, but I just chose to ignore it!

The real pattern, already forming then, was one of distraction and discouragement. My family's structure was no longer holding together; it was breaking down and falling apart like rotten wood, which could no longer be restored.

To rebuild a new structure in a different way required starting over again with fresh wood. Our lives are like rotting wood, but once we come to Christ, we are transformed into fresh new wood, becoming the structure that Christ can build upon! Thanks to God, I believe I'm much wiser at this time in my life!

Our Character Matters

One time, years ago, when I worked at a daycare, I was accused of hitting a child that I never even touched! I was suspended and not allowed to work with any children until it was cleared up! That really hurt me because I truly hadn't done anything wrong! Even though I was vindicated, because I really was innocent, it was hard to go back to work there. Now I felt like every time something happened to one of the children, I would be the first one considered a suspect. Our character does matter!

As far as my character is concerned, I'm asking God to take away anything that isn't pleasing to Him! I don't want to live in a way that people have to wonder who I am, where I'm one way in the public eye and another way when I'm behind closed doors. That's not to say that my life is based upon what other people think of me, but my character should be consistent. I don't want to be in and out or up and down on a rollercoaster of emotional instability.

Don't Rush Into Things

One of the most important lessons that I learned in my life was to no longer to rush into things! I rushed into many things I shouldn't have, missing out on things I could have had, if I had just waited. For instance, I believe that if I had waited until marriage to have sex, I would still have had my children, but they all would have had the same father. As the saying goes, "Good things come to those who wait"!

With wisdom, comes balance. We need to ask God for His wisdom and direction before rushing into things that might not even be meant for us. Life is a series of countless decisions that can take us in many different directions. Balance is needed to remain focused; I don't want to have to pull my thoughts back from a bunch of different directions! Sometimes our minds are like a speeding car, racing ahead with all kinds of thoughts and ideas that aren't productive, but we can't stop until we put on the brakes and refocus!

The principal of cause and effect is a relationship between events or things, where one is the result of the other. Simply stated, it's a matter of "if I do this, then that will happen". I have learned repeatedly that our choices really do make a difference in our journey through life! Before rushing into what could be a life-changing event, we need to stop and think about the outcome of that decision. There's no guarantee that life will be smooth sailing or that changes will be instantaneous, because there are always consequences to our actions that we'll have to work through. To back up and start over or take a detour to our destination can add unintended time, consequences, and wear and tear on us and those around us!

Just Be You

I always felt like I was extremely different. I just couldn't understand why so many people thought that something was wrong with me because I was so different. I believe that in order to become who we are ultimately meant to be, we can't be like everyone else.

To genuinely be myself hasn't always been easy, because it took a long time for me to truly realize who I am in Christ! Many times, it seemed like when I took a step forward, I would end up at a standstill or even go backwards. Becoming Christ like is a slow process and it takes work! It isn't instantaneous or something you miraculously receive out of a clear blue sky!

One of the hardest things for me to understand was that if I'm striving to be what I need to be in Christ, then it really doesn't matter what people think or say. There have been so many times in my life when others have said things about me, and I was worried about what they had said! I had completely forgotten that what God thinks about me is all that really matters; only His say so counts!

Be a Peacemaker

I received a message once from someone that I truly love telling me that I had said and done something that really hurt them. I'm not perfect by any means! At some point in time, I hope they realize that I would never deliberately hurt them, and I also pray that they'll forgive me!

I don't want to be the one who points the finger and places the blame on someone other than me. I want to be a peacemaker who comes up with positive solutions and makes things better, not worse!

Setting Goals

Until I met Jesus, I never had many long-term or even short-term goals in my life. I realized that with His help, I could now set and accomplish goals, and I could plan and go forward in my life, as well as in ministry!

I just want to clarify that I'm not against planning, but God doesn't want us to be extreme in what we do or how we go about doing it. Practically speaking, we still need to plan ahead when it comes to trips, weddings, and other events. Accommodations and weather conditions for those traveling are necessary and involve preparation.

Be Anxious for Nothing

Another lesson I learned was to do things one day at a time. Sometimes plans don't always work out. We should be anxious for nothing, although it's also a bitter revelation, when things aren't meant to be!

There were times in my life when I would wait for the phone or doorbell to ring, and even look out the window anxiously, waiting for a promise that was never intended to be kept! The return on ill-gotten things, whether it be money, material things, or even relationships, is zero or minus! I gained heartache, heartbreak, anger, rage, and disappointment. Doing and getting things the right way makes life so much better and worthwhile!

I'm still waiting for some things to manifest, but now I wait with expectation instead of being anxious.

Summary of My Life

"Therefore do not worry about tomorrow, for tomorrow will worry about itself. Each day has enough trouble of its own."
Matthew 6:34 (NIV)

I Wrote This for You!

As I summarize some of my life's experiences, I don't make light of them. I know there were a lot of things stuffed deep down inside of me for many years that were meant to come out. There are some personal moments, which at one point in my life, I couldn't share. I was more concerned about how I would be looked at, rather than how this book might make a difference in someone's life.

A lot of the things that I have written about in this book were meant to awaken a sense of awareness in the reader to the point that they wouldn't even consider putting themselves in harm's way when it comes to making decisions, especially when it comes to drug use and abusive relationships. For me, it was a time of utter despair and degradation! The damage inflicted can take years to reverse, and only God can heal that type of brokenness!

My hope is that my life lessons will lighten someone's load in all areas of their life; it will give others help and hope, so they are able to handle what they've been through or perhaps what they are still going through; and it may help them to realize that they too can have a quality of life, which they may not even have thought was possible.

I want to be a real inspiration to someone who really needs to be encouraged and motivated! I believe that there's someone, somewhere who needs to read this book. If you are reading this book now, just know that there's help from Jesus, who is our risen Savior. And if you don't have any of these issues, you may know someone who does. Please ask them to read this book; and hopefully, there's something in it that will help them!

Finding Peace

I have more peace in my life now than I've ever had, but that's not to say that I still don't get tested in many ways! But I now know who I am, who I serve, and also who will look out for me when things get a little rough or trying.

I thank God for all of the years that He has blessed me with to live so far, and I pray that He will bless me with many more! It has been very challenging at times, but all in all, I'm glad to still be in the land of the living!

Summary of My Life

"And we know that all things work together for good to those who love God, to those who are the called according to His purpose."

Romans 8:38 (NKJV)

Katrina Collins

The Weaver

My life is but a weaving
Between the Lord and me,
I cannot change the colors;
He worketh steadily.

Oft times He weaveth sorrow,
And I with tearful cries,
Forget I see from underneath;
He sees the upper side.

The dark threads are as needful
In the Weaver's skillful hand,
As the threads of gold and silver
In the patterns He has planned.

Not 'till the loom is silent
And the shuttles cease to fly,
Shall God unroll the canvas
And explain the reason why.

Author Unknown

Made in the USA
San Bernardino, CA
07 March 2016